Lincolnshire Railways

Compiled and written by
Stewart Squires

Published by Lincolnshire Books

All photographs copyright of Lincolnshire County Council
unless stated

First published in Great Britain by Lincolnshire Books
© 1998 Stewart Squire

ISBN: 1872375065

All rights reserved. No part of this publication may be reproduced, stored in a retrieval system, or transmitted in any form or by any means, electronic, mechanical, photocopying, recording or otherwise, without prior permission of the copyright holder.

Designed, typeset and produced for the publishers
by Graphics Unit, Lincolnshire County Council

Printed by G.W. Belton Ltd., Gainsborough, Lincs

LINCOLNSHIRE BOOKS
Official publishers to Lincolnshire County Council
County Offices
Newland
Lincoln LN1 1YL

CONTENTS

Number	Chapter	Page Number
	INTRODUCTION	i
1	NORTH LINCOLNSHIRE	1
2	LINCOLN	7
3	CENTRAL LINCOLNSHIRE	14
4	EAST LINCOLNSHIRE	17
5	GRANTHAM AREA	29
6	SOUTH LINCOLNSHIRE	35

INTRODUCTION

The invention of the railway was one of the greatest industrial feats of this country. It changed the way of life for people all over the world, in the vast majority of cases, for the better. Now, we take it for granted, but in the middle of the nineteenth century it was the wonder of the age.

Lincolnshire experienced these benefits too. For the first time, cheap travel for both goods and people opened up opportunities which were eagerly taken. There were social and employment changes, as well as physical alterations to the countryside.

Lincolnshire's first railway opened in August 1846. Within three years there were 200 miles in the County. That figure took 17 years to double, and another 18 years to treble. By 1877, 487 miles, 75% of the total, had been built, in 31 years. Within that period there were only eight years when no line opened, although construction was continuous. Imagine the outcry if it were proposed to build such a network today.

Since that time almost two thirds of that network has closed. Evidence of this survives in the buildings and civil engineering structures that remain. Perhaps the best legacy that these, and the lines still open, have left of their past, is in the collections of photographs that remain.

I have had the opportunity of putting together this collection of photographs from the stock held by the County Council within its libraries and museums. With them I have tried to illustrate many aspects of the railway scene in Lincolnshire, including the south bank of the Humber. Here you can follow both boom and bust; meet the people and see the buildings, engines, engine sheds and engineering; goods and coal trains and stations; high days and holidays; industry; accidents; and that aspect difficult to define, that today we call infrastructure. Finally, it also looks at the odd, the unusual, and the unique. A County of contrasts, its railways were also contrasting, a rich heritage to which I hope these photographs do justice and bring the reader some pleasure.

Stewart Squires

1 NORTH LINCOLNSHIRE

The station at Barton upon Humber was at the end of a short branch line from New Holland, opened in 1849, and seen here in July 1966. A suggestion, in 1911, to extend the line further west, to make a link with the North Lindsey Light Railway, and allow trains to run through to Scunthorpe, never came to fruition.

Of particular note is the open sided goods shed, a very unusual feature. Goods trains were withdrawn from 3 August 1970, but passenger trains still run, even though all of the buildings have been demolished. Trains link with buses here to provide a public service between Grimsby and Hull, over the Humber Bridge.

Barton upon Humber Station. Copyright PR White

One of the outcomes of the Railway Age was the development of Railway towns and villages. These were new communities built to house workers where there were no suitable existing settlements.

There was only one such place in Lincolnshire, at New Holland, on the south bank of the Humber.

Manchester Square, New Holland.

The Manchester, Sheffield and Lincolnshire Railway had its eastern terminus at New Holland. The reason was that it wanted to serve Hull, but was prevented by established railway interests from using the north bank. The next best was to use the south bank, and reach Hull by a ferry. Hence, a railway served pier was built out into the river, and a fleet of paddle steamers established the last link in the chain.

New Holland was only a very tiny community, with few facilities. Here, the railway built two stations, at both ends of the pier, a locomotive shed, and a dock, served by a network of sidings. For the benefit of their workers the Company built houses and a school. 43 of the houses were arranged around an open sided square, the south side of which is seen here. This was, and still is, called Manchester Square. The houses have been modernised, their windows, for example, not being the originals. Opposite to it, on the other side of the

NORTH LINCOLNSHIRE

road was Sheffield Terrace, both names derived from the name of the Company who built them.

Grimsby and Immingham Tramway.

opened a rural tramway with their link between Grimsby and the new port of Immingham. Such tramways were rare, and this one had many unique features. Because of the tidal nature of dock work, trams ran around the clock. Between the two towns, along the six mile route, were four intermediate stops, but no village, and very few residents. It was known locally as the "clickety", from the noise it made as the wheels ran over the rail joints.

The lower photograph shows car number 3, one of eight built by Brush for the opening of the line. Seen here before 1923, when the GCR became part of the

Grimsby and Immingham Tramway.

In 1912 the Great Central Railway

London and North Eastern Railway, it is in its original livery of brown, lined out with gold, with the GCR Coat of Arms on the front. These were the

NORTH LINCOLNSHIRE

longest trams in Britain, measuring 43 feet 8 inches in length. Number 3 lasted for the whole life of the line, being withdrawn for scrapping in 1961 when the tramway closed.

By the end of the Second World War the original trams were becoming worn out. In 1951, British Railways acquired seventeen trams from the Gateshead Tramway, becoming available when that tramway closed. These were much smaller than the original cars, and the upper view shows one of these, number 31, carrying on its side the BR "lion and wheel" totem, which was what a logo was called at that time. Built in 1925, this tram also survived until the closure of the tramway.

Northorpe Station. Copyright Sue Dickinson

Northorpe Station, on the line between Gainsborough and Barnetby, was built by the Manchester, Sheffield and Lincolnshire Railway, which later became the Great Central Railway. The building was a standard type, built also on the Lincoln to Barnetby line. This view was taken before World War One, looking towards Gainsborough.

It was very common, at this time, to pose such views for the photographer. Indeed, the cameras of the time could not cope with anything that moved. Here the engine, with a short goods train, is positioned on the level crossing. The train crew are standing on the outside of the engine, alongside the boiler. Next to the engine, on the other track, are three platelayers, with their trolley. Three staff and four ladies are on the platforms. Among the advertisements are those for Pears Soap, Epps's Cocoa, and Earles Cement.

The station here closed in 1955, but trains still pass, and both signal box and station buildings survive.

The Manchester, Sheffield and Lincolnshire Railway opened their line from Brigg to Gainsborough in 1849. On page 4 is their Gainsborough station, its architectural style harking back to the Georgian period. The grand entrance was replaced in 1904 by a much less dramatic subway, when sidings to serve the adjacent Marshalls Engineering Works were laid in the foreground. The platforms and track were covered by an overall roof, removed in 1921. This fine building was demolished in 1974, although the station is still open.

NORTH LINCOLNSHIRE

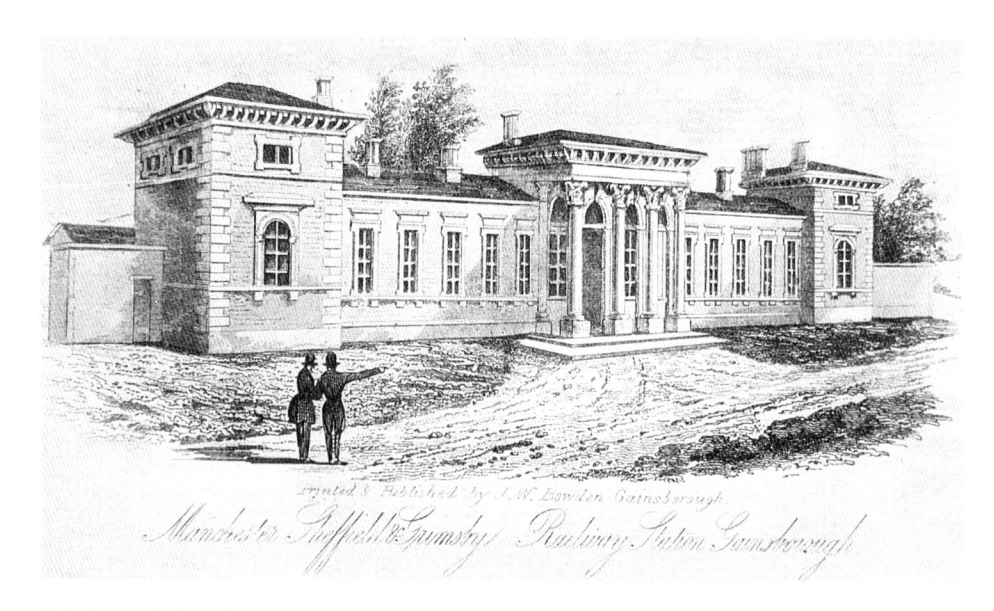

Gainsborough Central Station.

Such grand buildings were an expression of the wonders of the early Victorian age and the new form of travel, available to all. They were also designed to complement, and rival, the other public buildings in our towns, and Gainsborough has lost an architectural gem.

Gainsborough Lea Road Station.

Gainsborough's other station is on Lea Road, on the southern outskirts of the town. The line here opened in 1849 but this station was not ready on time, so the trains ran to the Manchester Sheffield and Lincolnshire Railway Station. The line to the south, to Sykes Junction at Saxilby, was built as a single line of rails. It had been doubled by 1858, by which time the Great Northern Railways Engineer was recommending it again be singled as an economy measure. The line cannot have been making a profit.

In preparation for the opening of the Gainsborough to Doncaster line, which would bring increased traffic, the line was closed from 1 December 1864 to be rebuilt. There were some steep gradients, the line at Lea for example, being lowered by twenty feet. It was reopened in 1867.

In the photograph, taken in 1905, the Booking Hall can be seen at street level, alongside the two storey Stationmaster's house. The station platforms and waiting rooms are on top of an embankment behind, and, to save weight, are of wooden construction.

Trent Junction, derailed goods train.

Trent Junction, derailed goods train.

Four routes converge on Gainsborough to utilise the bridge over the River Trent. They run to Lincoln, Doncaster, Sheffield and Grimsby. The line over the bridge was, therefore, once very much busier than it is today. To control the traffic two signalboxes were needed, one at each end, known as East Trent Junction and West Trent Junction. Their construction was unusual. The line was high on an embankment, and there was little room at the lineside, so both straddled the line on cast iron legs.

On 25 April 1913 a new signalbox on the east side of the bridge was brought into use to replace the two former ones. The reason for this was that East Trent box had been demolished shortly before in an accident. The immediate aftermath of that is shown here. A collision between two goods trains completely blocked the line. What the signalman felt as his world was turned upside down is not recorded.

Then, as now, an inquiry would be held into the causes and recommendations made to improve matters. Safety on the railway has always been of paramount importance.

Stationmasters at village stations often lived right on their station platform, with a bay window giving a view of the area so that he might not miss a customer coming or going. The house at Torksey did not follow that pattern, being set back slightly behind the platform, but he could still keep an eye on what was going on. The single storey building beyond is the Booking Office and Waiting Room.

Torksey Station. Copyright HB Priestley

Signals for both directions are "off", that is, allowing the passage of trains. Wayside signal boxes, such as the one seen on the left of the picture, would be only operated at busy periods. In between they would be "switched out".

When steam locomotives found it hard to get a grip on the rails, due to damp, or steep gradients, for example, sand would be run onto the rail in front of their wheels from a small hopper on the engine. Such sand had to be very fine and suitable sources were a godsend to railway companies if one could be found adjacent to their own property. The Great Central Railway, who operated this line, found such a supply here, behind the platform on the left, and quarried it from 1897.

The line through Torksey closed in 1959, because of the poor state of the Torksey Bridge, over the River Trent, about half a mile beyond the station. The line reopened, to serve an oil terminal on the Torksey bank of the river, in 1966, but closed again in 1988.

2 LINCOLN

Although entitled Lincoln from the Great Northern Railway, this engraving of 1852 actually shows a train on the Manchester, Sheffield and Lincolnshire Railway. It has crossed the bridge over the River Witham, east of Stamp End Lock. The line here, to Market Rasen and Barnetby, opened in 1848.

The bridge itself perhaps looks to be nothing out of the ordinary. It was built to a design of William Fairbairn, his Patent Girder Bridge. It was such a success that it became a standard adopted worldwide. What makes the Lincoln Bridge special is that it is now the oldest surviving example and is still in use.

Lincoln from Great Northern Railway.

The boat is a steam packet, an example of the boats which provided a passenger service between Lincoln and Boston. Its funnel is being raised after being lowered to pass under the bridge. The Great Northern Railway built its Lincoln Boston line along the river bank between the two towns and so became a direct competitor for this traffic. This line, too, opened in 1848 and a price war ensued between boats and trains. It was one the boats could not win, mainly because of the far shorter journey times of the train, and the passenger boats were driven off the water by 1863.

Lincoln St Marks

The distinction of being the first railway in the County falls to the line from Nottingham to Lincoln, which was opened on 3 August 1846, by the Midland Railway. For two years the station in Lincoln, adjacent to the High Street, was a terminus, until the level crossing in the foreground was created. Here it made an end on junction with the Manchester, Sheffield and Lincolnshire line to Barnetby. The latter used the Midland Station for passengers, but each company had its own goods sidings, one set on each side of the road.

Until the railways were nationalised in 1947 both Lincoln stations were owned by different companies, but both called Lincoln. British Railways ended any confusion for passengers by renaming

LINCOLN

the station Lincoln St Marks, after a nearby church now demolished, from 25 September 1950.

It became the City's main station in 1965, when the through trains to London were diverted into it with the closure of the direct Lincoln to Grantham line. This photograph was taken on 11 December 1976 immediately before the level crossing gates were replaced by lifting barriers.

The last trains ran from here on 11 May 1985, from when railway facilities were rationalised in Lincoln, with services concentrated on the Central Station. The fine main buildings here still survive, having been incorporated into the new shopping development on the site.

Getting Water, Lincoln Typhoid Epidemic, 1905.

The story of the Lincoln Typhoid Epidemic in 1904 and 1905 is well known. The pollution of the City's water supply led to widespread suffering and 131 deaths. The short term solution was to increase local supplies, from new boreholes, and in the long term, bring an entirely new supply from Elkesley in Nottinghamshire, via a pipeline 22 miles long.

Before any of this could happen, however, people still needed water. They were told to boil all water for ten minutes to make it safe. At the same time, water was brought in from outside by rail.

Alderman Smith, of Newark, arranged for a free supply from that town. It was pumped into surplus engine tenders and brought to Lincoln by the Midland Railway, again free of charge. At St Marks householders were invited to collect it themselves.

This photograph shows the townspeople fetching the clean water in their buckets and watering cans. By the end of 1904 the situation in Lincoln had eased and this supply ceased. However, following problems with the filtration beds, it had to be resumed for a short time the next year.

In 1911 the country's railway network was brought to a standstill by a national railway strike. It was a very bad tempered affair, with riots in Liverpool resulting in two deaths. The Government took a very confrontational view and the Home Secretary, Winston Churchill, called in the troops to protect railway property.

LINCOLN

Guardian of Law & Order, Railway Strike Lincoln, 1911.

Lincoln did not escape the unrest. Railway property, and local businesses, had windows smashed and buildings set on fire. Here, at the Midland Railway Station, later St Marks, a sergeant of the Militia is on duty, with rifle and fixed bayonet. The troops were quartered in a railway carriage. Many people today think we live in a more lawless age than ever before. It is hard to believe, therefore, that in the 20th Century, in a time of peace, we once had armed soldiers on the streets, on duty to control the local populace.

In addition to excursion trains provided by the railways themselves to take people to the seaside, and other places of interest, there are those arranged by firms to take their workers away for the day. Works outings are almost as old as the railways themselves. The very first recorded example was in 1840, when the Newcastle engineers, R and W Hawthorn, hired a train from Newcastle to Carlisle and return.

Outings became particularly popular from the later years of the 19th Century. Travel was often free for workers, with their family and friends travelling at cost. They were an excellent way to promote good staff relations. The seaside was a popular destination, and resorts such as Blackpool, Great Yarmouth and Scarborough boomed.

Here, on 10 October 1936 is the special train organised by Robeys, of Lincoln, to Blackpool. Smartly turned out workers and a special headboard for the engine are typical of the time. Despite what appears to have been a recent downpour, no doubt everyone enjoyed a trip to see the famous illuminations.

On 14 May 1959, a special train is seen here leaving Lincoln Central Station. This was chartered by the Institute of Water Engineers, to run from Lincoln to Driffield and travelled via Doncaster, Selby and Market Weighton. The engine was 4-6-0, Class B12/3, 61577, loaned for the trip by Cambridge shed. One of very few survivors of the Class, this was one of its last duties, as it was scrapped later that year.

Lincoln - Robey Annual Outing to Blackpool 1936

4-6-0 Steam Locomotive, No. 61577 passing through Lincoln Central.

LINCOLN

The classification of steam locomotives relates to the type and design of the engine. In this case the wheel grouping, 4-6-0, shows that there are four leading wheels, six driving wheels, and no trailing wheels. B12 is the locomotive class given to these engines by the LNER. A B12/1 was the original Great Eastern Railway Class, introduced in 1911. The B12/2 was a development of the type, with different valves. The B12/3 was a rebuild of some of the the original locos, from 1943, with a round topped boiler. This clearly shows the very long life that a steam locomotive could have and engines would often be rebuilt, especially when money was tight, as it was cheaper than designing and building new.

Society, in addition to running their famous model railway at their clubrooms in the town, are also well known for the trips out by train that they organised for many years. This is one of those. On 12 October 1963, a tour took place of branch lines in Nottinghamshire and South Yorkshire. Retford engine, O4 Class 63585, is seen here at Platform 7 at Lincoln Central Station, prior to setting out.

This Class of loco was built in great numbers for the Great Central Railway. During the First World War more than 500 were built for use by the military in France. Put to use on Britain's railways afterwards, many were again sent abroad in the Second World War. In 1952, five were sent to the Suez War Department Depot, and did not return.

The Branch line tour was one of the last duties for 63585, as she was condemned on 19 December 1963.

Engine No.63585, at Lincoln Central Station, 12th October 1963.

The Gainsborough Model Railway

There were four railway engine sheds and depots in the Lincoln area. The Great Eastern Railway at Pyewipe Junction, the Midland at St Marks, the

LINCOLN

Great Northern at East Holmes and the Great Central at Pelham Street. With first the Grouping and then nationalisation, the number was reduced and the former Great Northern shed became the City's principal depot.

Coaling Plant for Steam Locos, Lincoln Holmes Sidings, circa 1960.

This photograph shows the mechanised coaling plant, on the Holmes, to the west of the Shed. This was a typical improvement, at loco sheds nationwide, installed in the 1930s and built of reinforced concrete, as were so many buildings of that era.

Coal wagons would be tipped at the base, the coal falling into a bunker. From here, a hoist carried coal up into the main part of the structure. Locomotives then filled their tenders with coal by positioning themselves underneath. Prior to their introduction coaling was a backbreaking job, usually being done by hand.

The plant must have become a big asset for, in 1937, there were 50 locomotives stationed here. At least in Lincoln there were no houses cheek by jowl with the shed to suffer the polluting effects of the thick clouds of smoke which were associated with such sheds.

The Smith - Clayton Forge was one of Lincoln's main engineering works. Its Abbey Works was alongside the Lincoln to Market Rasen line, east of the Power Station. Like Lincoln's other great firms, it was rail connected and used its own locomotives within its premises.

Loco at Smith Clayton Forge.

The Forge previously used two steam locomotives but, in 1961, they purchased a Ruston loco from their fellow City manufacturers. This was one of the 88DS Class, one of their most successful designs. No less than 254 were built, most to standard gauge, but also to seven other gauges, from 3 feet to 5 feet 6 inches, for use on railways worldwide. In November 1986, as it

LINCOLN

was by then redundant, it was moved to the Museum of Lincolnshire Life, shortly after this photograph was taken.

Crane Tank, that is a conventional steam tank engine which carried a crane jib. In 1903 Robeys rebuilt it in this form as a shunting locomotive. No buyer could be found, so it is believed to have been used by them as their own works shunter.

Robey Loco, circa 1899.

Victorian engineers were very versatile, if they could identify a market they would consider building for it. The rapid expansion of the railway network in the second half of the nineteenth century generated a growing need for railway locomotives, not only for the railway companies, but also for the multitude of companies who had their own railway sidings. These included factories, mines and quarries, depots, gas works and institutions, and it was for them that Robeys, of Lincoln, built a number of steam locomotives from 1870.

The one shown here was not built originally by them. They acquired it from an unknown source as an 0-4-0

Thorpe on the Hill Level Crossing House.

This delightful building owes its design to the picturesque style, looking more akin to the lodge gatehouse of a country estate than a railway station. The Midland Railway built this, and other buildings with similar styles for its line into Lincoln in 1846, and those that still survive are probably the best surviving examples of early railway architecture in the East Midlands. Although the station here closed for passengers on 7 February 1955 and goods on 15 June 1964, the line is still open and the building survives.

3 CENTRAL LINCOLNSHIRE

A busy scene at Wragby Station, in Edwardian days, as a train from Bardney to Louth disgorges its passengers.

Original Bardney timber Railway Bridge, replaced by present bridge in 1860.

Wragby Station in GNR Days. Copyright A Turner

This line opened in 1874, being built by the Louth and Lincoln Railway Co. Wragby was the only one of the lines stations to have two platforms, which enables us to tell in which direction this train was heading. Other stations on the line, those at South Willingham and Donington on Bain, had exactly the same design of station building. Three years later, in 1877, the Louth and East Coast Railway opened their line from Louth to Mablethorpe. The Louth and East Coast Railway built their stations at Grimoldby, Saltfleetby, Theddlethorpe and Mablethorpe to exactly the same design. They were built by different contractors and had different Boards of Directors. However, there was obviously some connection, even if only that the Louth and East Coast simply bought their station design, and thereby saved some money, from their earlier neighbour.

When the Lincolnshire Loop Line, between Boston and Lincoln opened in 1848, it was part of the main railway route from London to the north. North of Bardney Station, the line crossed the River Witham by this fine timber bridge. Timber was a common material for bridges and viaducts on early railways. The Bardney bridge did not last for long. After a fire on a timber bridge elsewhere on the system the GNR determined to replace them all and this was replaced by an iron structure, opening in 1860.

There is a fine scale model of this original bridge in the National Railway Museum in York.

Bardney Station, as the nameboard proudly proclaims, was the junction on the Lincoln to Boston line, where one could change for the Louth to Bardney line. In this Victorian photograph, the staff are standing on what was the Louth line platform. When the station first opened, this platform served Boston trains. The opening of the Louth line in 1874 required alterations and, as a result, an island platform was built for the through trains and this one shortened to serve those on the branch.

to give itself a modern image at that time.

For a short period, 1848 to 1852, Bardney found itself on the main railway route from London to the north. It lost this status when the present day main line was opened between Peterborough, Grantham, Newark and Doncaster.

Bardney Railway Station. Copyright G Benton

The architecture of the buildings was of the very distinctive Great Northern Railway style. Many Lincolnshire stations were of this, albeit each one would have small variations. Colloquially, they are known as the "tower" type, as their main and common feature is a square, three storey tower for the stationmaster to live in. It has wide overhanging eaves, arched windows and tall chimneys. This Italianate style was all the rage in the 1840s and 50s and, no doubt, the GNR wanted

Bardney Sugar Beet Factory Loco.

In 1927 a sugar beet factory was established between Bardney Station and the River Witham. This was an ideal location as beet could be delivered to the factory by road, rail and water. There were an extensive array of sidings here as beet and coal were delivered, and empty wagons and beet pulp were despatched, often several times a day.

The factory needed its own shunting locomotive to move wagons around the works. Initially steam locomotives were used, but were replaced by a diesel in 1954 and this is shown on page 15. It was a Ruston and Hornsby 165DS Class, built in the Boultham Works in Lincoln in 1954, and delivered new to Bardney in that year. The British Sugar Corporation had great faith in these locomotives, no less than sixteen being purchased in 1953 and 54, working at fourteen of their sugar factories throughout the east of England. This locomotive worked at the Bardney factory until rail traffic to the works ceased in 1981.

The next station south of Bardney was at Southrey. Seen here in this pre 1900 view it is typical of other similar stations on the Great Northern Railway in Lincolnshire, serving small villages.

Southrey.

CENTRAL LINCOLNSHIRE

This design was also seen at Stixwould, the next station on southwards, and at Surfleet between Spalding and Boston.

The level crossing here gave access to the bank of the River Witham and the ferry across to Dunston Fen. The horse muck shows that this has recently been used. A two storey Stationmaster's House was provided, detached from these buildings, to the left of the level crossing gate.

Ruston loco at Southrey.

As a direct contrast to permanent railways, Lincolnshire also had an example of a peripatetic railway. The Lincolnshire River Board had the responsibility of maintaining rivers and drains throughout the County. In Lincolnshire good drainage is of paramount importance in maintaining farm production. However, not all the waterways were conveniently near to roads. The Board maintained a stock of narrow gauge railway equipment, all of which was portable, so that materials could be transported between road and working site. The suitability of narrow gauge railways for transport over boggy ground had been proved during the First World War.

Of 2 foot gauge, a stock of rails, side tipping wagons and four locomotives were kept in the depot near to Southrey Station. The locomotives were all built by Rustons, at their Boultham Works in Lincoln. 2, delivered in 1936, were of the 18/21 HP Class with 2 more, LA Class but very similar, in 1959. One of the latter, Works Number 421432, was rescued for the Museum of Lincolnshire Life after the stock was declared redundant and may be seen in the Museum today. It is pictured here at Southrey Depot before its removal.

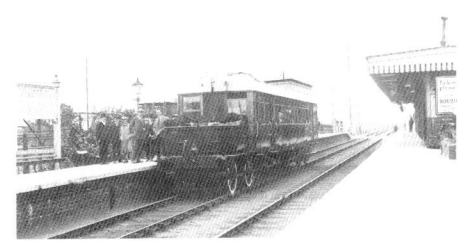

Clayton Experimental Loco, Woodhall Junction. Copyright P. Lobley

Public Conveniences, Kirkstead.

The Clayton Wagon Works, of Lincoln, built eleven railcars for the London and North Eastern Railway, ten in 1928 and the first a year earlier. The latter is seen on page 17 on a trial run at Woodhall Junction, on 3 July 1927. Numbered at this time 41 and later renumbered 2121, it was named Pilot, like all the others, after famous stage coaches. 41 was different to its stable mates, in having an all teak livery and round, instead of oblong, buffers. The railcar spent much of its life in the north east of England, based at Heaton shed, from where it was scrapped in 1936. They were never a great success, often out of work with engine and boiler problems.

This station became a junction in 1855 when the branch line to Horncastle opened, although it was called Kirkstead until renamed in July 1922. It was different to many other county stations in that it lost its passenger trains, in 1970, before its goods trains. Goods trains ran from Lincoln to Horncastle until April 1971.

The second photograph shows a close up view of a structure just out of view to the left on the first photograph. This is a very ornate cast iron gentlemen's urinal, at the back edge of the platform, shown as it was after the station had closed. A very necessary convenience and unique in Lincolnshire. Made in Glasgow in 1880, it is now housed at the Museum of Lincolnshire Life, in Lincoln, where it may be seen today - but not used!

Dogdyke. Copyright Alan Rundle

There were few bridges over the River Witham, between Lincoln and Boston. Because of this, several of the railway stations on the east bank of the railway line that followed the river, were connected to the west by ferries. This is Dogdyke Ferry in 1910. The large pontoon type boats were used for carts and animals, whereas people on foot were taken across in the rowing boat. The railway station is in the background, the goods shed partly hidden by the trees.

This station was unusual in that the villages which it served, Dogdyke and Chapel Hill, were on the west bank. The other stations served villages on the east bank, with the ferries linking fenland farms to the west with the trains. This is likely to have made the Dogdyke ferry the most used.

Dogdyke had only a small goods yard with two public sidings, one of which ran through the goods shed. It had two other sidings. One, off the photograph to the left, served a corn mill. The other, tantalisingly just out of view to the right, adjacent to the ferry, served a small wharf on the river. This was very unusual for Lincolnshire stations and was reached by a wagon turntable.

The line here was closed on 17 June 1963 and two years later the station buildings were burned down.

The evidence can be seen in the wide platforms, with the buildings linked to the platform edge by wide awnings.

The natural route of the line here lay further to the east. It was probably pushed to the west by the concern of the Marquess of Ripon, who lived at Nocton Hall about one mile away, and the Hall would have been adversely

Nocton and Dunston Station. Copyright G Benton

By the time that the Great Northern and Great Eastern Railway opened its section of line between Sleaford and Lincoln, including Nocton and Dunston Station, in 1882, most of the County's railway network was complete. This was a secondary main line, linking East Anglia and the South Yorkshire Coalfield. This was a small village station, but was built with a spacious feeling very different to the cramped nature of many early village stations.

affected by a line closer to the village. Because it cut through the dip slope of the Lincoln Heath at this point, expensive cuttings were required.

Another effect was that the station was further away from the village that it might have been. It has been said that if a station had two village names in its title, it would be convenient for neither. However, here both villages were about half a mile away, a matter of little consequence in those late Victorian days.

CENTRAL LINCOLNSHIRE

Metheringham Station. Copyright Paul Slater

The next station south of Nocton and Dunston was Blankney and Metheringham. In September 1961 it was one of 25 Lincolnshire stations which lost its passenger trains. This was before Beeching, but it was affected by the Beeching cuts as on 15 June 1964 it lost its goods trains. On this day 106 stations nationwide closed, including 8 goods yards in the County.

However, in October 1975 it regained its station when the platforms seen in the background were built. Reopened as Metheringham, oddly, the signal box is still called Blankney as this 1990 view shows. The building which can just be seen with a flat roof behind the left hand platform was built during the Second World War. It was the Train Control office, which would have taken the place of that in Lincoln if the latter had been bombed. Train Control was the centre which monitored train movements and it was connected by phone to all parts of its area.

Ruskington Station, 1908.

20

CENTRAL LINCOLNSHIRE

When the line opened Henry Chaplin lived at Blankney Hall. He was an MP, landowner, racehorse owner and friend of the Prince of Wales, later Edward VII. The Prince was a regular visitor to lavish parties at Blankney Hall, and to the Blankney Hunt. Chaplin connected the Hall direct to the station with a Coach Road. This can still be seen passing under a road on the edge of Blankney where the bridge can easily be mistaken for a railway bridge.

The view of Ruskington Station is of about 1908, and shows the station staff. One of the major benefits that railways brought to rural areas was alternative employment opportunities. Prior to this men worked on the land, took up a rural craft; a wheelwright for example, or went into trade. The railways not only provided secure employment and regular wages but also opportunities for promotion.

The men shown here would be the porters, booking office and goods clerks, signalmen, permanent way and signal inspectors, messenger and deliveryman. Even a village station such as this provided for these fifteen men. In addition to these would be those employed by the local coal merchant, based in the sidings.

This line, between Lincoln and Sleaford, was opened in 1882. That section south from Ruskington was built by the Sleaford contractors Kirk and Parry. The firm built several railways, but few in Lincolnshire. They did not build the stations, however, another contractor, Pattinsons, being given that contract.

Sleaford Water Tank.

CENTRAL LINCOLNSHIRE

This station closed for passengers in 1961, and for goods in 1964. A new station was built on the same site and reopened on 5 May 1975.

A good supply of both coal and water are a prerequisite for the successful operation of steam engines. Coal was provided at sheds and depots, but water was more universally available. A water crane could be sited adajacent to the track, anywhere that a good supply was available and in a place where an engine would normally stop.

On page 21, at the west end of the platform at Sleaford, near to the level crossing,is the water tank and crane at the time when it was being demolished. This is of an unusual design, rarely seen in Lincolnshire. Water cranes, that is the structure below the tank, were very common, with the cranes being supplied with water from a separate water tank nearby. The arm swung out at right angles when in use, with the flexible pipe, or "bag" as it was known, providing the connection to the tender.

Two other items of interest are the "20" sign, seen in reverse, on the platform in front of the buildings, indicating a 20 mph speed limit over the level crossing, and the telephone pole to the right of the tank. Wires were part of the railway scene, carrying the telephone links between stations and signalboxes along the route.

Rauceby Station. Copyright M. A. King

Occasionally, a station survives almost in a timewarp and it can be difficult to date a photograph. One of these was photographed at Rauceby in 1987. It has a very distinctive Great Northern Railway atmosphere, with level crossing gates, signal box, house, waiting room with canopy, garden, lamps, and signal post all evoking the period of 100 years before.

The line here, between Sleaford and Grantham, opened in 1857. Rauceby Station did not open until 1st October 1881. The goods sidings were closed in 1964, with station staff being taken away from 1968. Passenger trains still call, however.

4 EAST LINCOLNSHIRE

The station at Louth was designed by Weightman and Hadfield for the East Lincolnshire Railway and built in 1847/48. It is of the Tudor Gothic style, seen here to its greatest advantage from its approach from the road. The other side, with the platforms, did not appear quite so grand largely because for much of its life the elevation was hidden by an all over roof and latterly, a conventional canopy.

Louth Station.

The building is a good example of the lengths that Victorian railways went to impress travellers. Grand enough to impress the local landed gentry, imagine how excited ordinary people were to be able to pass through such fine portals. It was an experience new to many of them, denied such opportunities at similarly grand, privately owned houses.

The canopied arcade in front of the main entrance is a "porte - cochere". Into this would be driven those who arrived in horse drawn vehicles, especially if it was wet, so that they may enter the station in the dry.

Closed to passengers in 1970, the site was abandoned after the last goods trains called here in 1980. Badly vandalised by 1987, an application was made to demolish it, by now a listed building. Permission was refused and happily, it was subsequently converted to flats and its future is now secure.

Alford was one of the principal stations on the East Lincolnshire Railway and marked out as such by having an all over roof between the platforms, as were the stations at Louth and Firsby. The roof at Alford was removed and replaced by the rather utilitarian awning seen here in 1970.

The station was known simply as Alford until 1923. On 1st July of that year it was renamed to avoid any confusion with the only other station in Britain with the same name, a station in the north of Scotland, west of Aberdeen. It would be interesting to speculate that this came about as a result of travellers becoming confused and finding themselves a very long way away from

Alford Station. Copyright Peter Grey

where they really wanted to go. The reason is, however, very simple. In 1923 the two companies who owned the two Alford Stations, The Great Northern Railway, and The Great North of Scotland Railway, were combined, with many others, into the London and North Eastern Railway and it was they who needed to make the distinction.

The Lincoln typhoid epidemic has been referred to in the section on Lincoln. In addition to a temporary supply being provided from Newark, water was also provided from a borehole at Willoughby. Here, in 1905,

a Great Northern Railway train of water tenders is standing in the station with loco 191, a standard goods engine, to a design by Patrick Stirling, at its head.

Willoughby Station, A Train of water tenders, Lincoln Typhoid Epidemic 1905. Copyright Mrs J Metheringham

Willoughby was the junction for the line to Sutton on Sea and Mablethorpe and the train is standing in the Mablethorpe bay platform. This was a new station built in 1886, with the line to Sutton, replacing an earlier station built forty years before. This had been south of the station level crossing. The Great Northern, ever looking to save money, built it to the same plans that they were using for London suburban stations and so this location resembled a small piece of the capital, lost in the wilds of Lincolnshire.

The bracket signal, immediately to the right of the station canopy, carries at its

EAST LINCOLNSHIRE

highest point the signal for the main line to Louth and Grimsby. The lower arm is the signal for the branch line. They are both at Danger, or in the "on" position. To the rear of the train a signal is in the "off" position. This is a Great Northern Railway somersault signal, which pivoted at its centre. This was a design very common in Lincolnshire, but which is now very rare indeed.

Mablethorpe Station. Copyright Mr Lansdell-Welfare

Railway views were a popular subject for postcards around the turn of the century. This one, of Mablethorpe Station, shows locomotive No 703 arriving with a train from Louth. The fashions of the people standing on the platform date this to Edwardian times, on a summers day.

Mablethorpe Station building was little different to the other stations on the line to Louth. However, its large awning gave it an air of authority over the others. Above the awning can be seen the signal box. This had an unusual siting. Signal boxes are usually located alongside the running lines, with a good view in either direction. At Mablethorpe, however, it was cut off from the lineside by a bay platform, the signalman crossing the siding by a timber bridge spanning the gap between the box steps and the platform. With the bay occupied the bridge had to be removed. The signal box had to be built as a tall structure to ensure that the signalman had a view of the station over any trains and the adjacent buildings.

Mablethorpe had four platforms, two in the centre for through trains, and two bays. It was perhaps ironic that both bays faced north, whereas most trains came in from the south. This was a legacy of the early days, when the Louth direction was the principal route. As holiday traffic grew and more trains came from the Midlands, the southern route, from Willoughby, increased in importance.

Mablethorpe Station. Copyright A Turner

Mablethorpe owes its popularity and development to its railway. Every summer thousands of holidaymakers passed over its station platforms. For most of its life, over 100,000 people a year used its trains, the peak year being 1936, with 166,000. The highest number of excursion trains visiting on one day was on August Bank Holiday Sunday in 1951, with no less than nineteen.

In the second view on page 25 a solid mass of passengers are heading for the sands. They carry no luggage, so are daytrippers. The date of the photograph is not known, other than it was between the Wars. A clue lies in a very rare view of Mablethorpe Engine Shed, visible above the train, to the right of the signal post. This was closed in 1924 when Louth loco shed took over the responsibility for providing engines for the regular branch trains.

In 1926 the Spilsby branch train is leaving Firsby Station, which can be seen in the background of the photograph below. 4537 was the usual branch engine and could be seen in the area right into the 1940s. These engines, classified as C12 by the LNER, were originally built for London suburban services and when that duty became too arduous, because of the increasing size of their trains, they worked for most of their lives in rural areas. Many came to Lincolnshire where they could be seen on all of the East Lincolnshire lines. 4537, later 7387, and finally, under British Railways, 67387, came to the County in 1921.

A Spilsby train at Firsby 1926. Copyright Hallgarth Collection

EAST LINCOLNSHIRE

Staff at Spilsby Railway Station. Copyright Hallgarth Collection

The branch line from Firsby to Spilsby was opened in 1868. This view, with the station platform in the background, shows a fine Great Northern Railway locomotive on which much loving care has been spent, probably by some of the station staff who posed next to it. 126 was one of a batch of 13 engines built at Doncaster, by the GNR, in 1868. An 0-4-2 Well Tank, to the design of Patrick Stirling, when new it worked in the West Riding. They were used on both passenger and goods trains.

Spilsby.

This is a photograph of a painting, taken from a photograph. On the original are a number of features missing from the painting, including a

EAST LINCOLNSHIRE

tall signal, and three men and a horse. It is believed to have been taken in 1869.The engine is one of the first built for the GNR between 1847 and 1849. With its distinctive 4 wheel coaches, it is a rare illustration of what the trains of the time looked like. The engine was No 33A, a 2-2-2, built by Sharp Roberts and Co. known as "Little Sharps".

Wainfleet Station. Copyright Mr Lansdell-Welfare

The line to Wainfleet, from Firsby, was opened in 1871. It was a terminus until the extension through to Skegness opened on 28 July 1873. This is an early view of Wainfleet Station in the 1880s, with the branch train approaching from Firsby. Note the railway track. It was common at this time for the sleepers to be completely covered over by the ballast.

At this time the branch was single track. On the extreme left of the picture is the goods dock and the wall of the goods shed. Both of these were replaced within the goods sidings when the whole line was doubled in 1900 and a second platform built here. To the left of the station buildings, in the background, can be seen the engine shed, which was closed in the 1940s.

Arrival of the London excursion at Skegness Station, 1910.

The Great Northern Railway reached the coast only in Lincolnshire. With the reductions in working hours, bank holidays and annual summer holidays that became the right of the working man in the later years of the 19th century, trips to the seaside became increasingly popular. The GNR brought holidaymakers to the coast from London, Nottinghamshire and South Derbyshire, and the resorts of Skegness and Mablethorpe developed as a result.

This photograph, taken in 1910, shows GNR Large Atlantic, 1427, shortly after arrival at Skegness with an excursion from Kings Cross.

5 GRANTHAM AREA

Belton Signalbox was to the north of Peasecliff Tunnel on the main line between Grantham and Barkston. It was closed in 1922, but is seen here with a southbound Great Northern express. The signals are on very tall posts to enable engine drivers to see them clearly against the sky.

The logical route for this line north of Grantham would have been to follow the River Witham. However, Lord Brownlow objected to the line coming into sight of his home, Belton House and so the Great Northern Railway were forced to a route further to the west. This incurred greater cost and delay to opening because of the tunnel and its associated earthworks.

Belton Signalbox.

Grantham Shed.

Grantham Shed.

29

GRANTHAM AREA

Diamond Jubilee.

Grantham was an important place on the Great Northern Railway. The main line from London to the north ensured that it had, and continues to have, express services. As it was at a convenient point on the line, 105 miles from Kings Cross, for trains to change their engines, and the junction for services to Leicester, Nottingham, Lincoln and Sleaford, it always had an important engine shed. The shed was home to a variety of goods and passenger locomotives, including those which were used on the crack express trains of the day.

The two views on page 29 show Great Northern Railway locomotives standing by the front of the engine shed. Both include groups of workers, probably fitters, engine cleaners and other maintenance staff, and were taken before the formation of the London and North Eastern Railway in 1922.

1303 was a Class D2 4-4-0 secondary express loco, to a design of HA Ivatt, built in the late 1860s. It would have been used mainly on trains on the branch lines radiating from Grantham. It is standing over one of the inspection pits, which enabled those parts of the engine, normally difficult to get at, to be maintained.

1401 was a GNR 4-4-2 Large Atlantic, one of 80 built between 1904 and 1908 for main line trains. No. 251 of this

GRANTHAM AREA

Class has been preserved and can be seen today in the National Railway Museum. Engine sheds were notoriously dirty places to work in, but these photographs do show that high standards of cleanliness, to both engines and the site, were maintained.

The third photograph moves forward to the London and North Eastern Railway, and one of the famous classes of express engines. 4-6-2 Pacific, Diamond Jubilee was built at Doncaster in 1924. It was rebuilt into its form as illustrated in 1941, one of the Class A3 engines, of which "Flying Scotsman" is the most famous, and only surviving, example. Diamond Jubilee was stationed at Grantham for a number of years in the 1930`s. In 1959 it returned, by then carrying its British Railways number, 60046 and remained here, apart from a brief transfer to New England, Peterborough, during late 1962 and early 1963, until it was withdrawn from service in 1963.

The LNER used the names of famous racehorses for many of the locomotives in this Class. This was very appropriate as they were the racehorses of the East Coast Main Line. "Diamond Jubilee" was foaled in 1897 and owned by the Prince of Wales. In 1900 he won the Triple Crown, (the Two Thousand Guineas, the Derby and the St Leger).

Grantham's first Railway Station.

Grantham's first railway station, seen here in 1951, was used by travellers for only a very short time. The Ambergate Station, as it was known, was opened for business on 15 July 1850. It was at the wharf, where the Grantham Canal ended, and was one terminus of the grandly named Ambergate, Nottingham and Boston and Eastern Counties Junction Railway. This company built only the central portion of its proposed line, between Nottingham and Grantham.

From 1852 trains ran into the Great Northern Station when it opened and the Ambergate Station was left to serve as a goods yard for many years. It was appropriate that canal and railway terminus should be adjacent to each other. Both linked the same two towns and the canal wharf was where Grantham traders had become established on the west edge of the town. Furthermore, the railway company took over the Canal in 1854. This was a sensible move. It was not the intention to close the latter, more to ensure that there was sensible trading and one did not steal the trade of the other if it was more appropriate to the goods carried.

Above and below Dysart Road Coal Wharf.

The main goods traffic to the Ambergate Station was coal. Indeed, the sidings adjacent to the canal wharf were known as the Coal Wharf by the railway company. Sidings served the needs of the Grantham Gas, Light and Coal Co., established adjacent to the canal in 1832, as well as a number of local coal merchants. These two photographs show the carts and wagons of two, WH Garton and Co. and H Bowman and Co.

GRANTHAM AREA

Note that in both cases the vehicles are shown in spotless condition. They were probably taken for publicity purposes, that of Gartons certainly.

Both merchants prominently display their name on the side of their railway wagons. These were their privately owned wagons and dedicated to carry coal to their yard from whichever colliery they dealt with. At this time, before the First World War, most wagons were privately owned. The system was inherently inefficient, as the railways had to sort trains more frequently, to ensure they were used only on their owner's business, both when full and empty. This was not the case with wagons in common use which could be used on all routes.

In 1897 the yard was dealing with 6 trains a day, with 3 goods, mostly coal, coming in and 3 trains of empties being despatched.

Hornsby's Packing Shop, Grantham.

GRANTHAM AREA

One of Grantham's major manufacturers was the firm of Richard Hornsby and Sons Ltd, at their Spittlegate Iron Works. The previous photograph shows the interior of their Packing and Forwarding Shop, which was opened on 1 March 1905. The shop contains a small selection of their products at that time, mostly agriculture related, reapers, root choppers and a Patent Hedge Cutter.

Like most large engineering works, the works was alongside a railway and was served by its own sidings. Not only that, but the Company also operated their own locomotives within their premises. Over the years they had three one of which can be seen on the centre left of the picture. This was an 0-4-0 Saddle Tank, built by Andrew Barclay Sons and Co Ltd of Kilmarnock, delivered new to the works in 1882 and scrapped on site in the 1950s.

High Dyke, on the main line five miles south of Grantham, was the junction with one of the County's ironstone railways. The branch from here to Colsterworth was opened in 1918 and extended to Stainby shortly after. For 45 years the junction sidings were a familiar sight to travellers, immediately adjacent to the north portal of Stoke Tunnel.

The iron ore was despatched to the Scunthorpe steelworks. Here, on the day before the branch was closed, 5 September 1963, a Class O2 2-8-0 brings a loaded train off the branch. In the background, to the left of the tender, the engine waiting to take the load on to Scunthorpe, 2-8-0, 90169, can be seen. This was one of over 700 engines built during the Second World War for the War Department and subsequently taken over by British Railways. To its left is the mouth of Stoke Tunnel.

Class O2 2-8-0 at High Dyke 5th September 1963.

6 SOUTH LINCOLNSHIRE

When the line through South Witham was constructed a bed of limestone some 60 feet thick was revealed adjacent to the station. In this view, looking west towards Saxby, the resultant limestone quarry, opened in 1907, is to the right of the line beyond the goods shed. Because the line here was carried on an embankment, the quarry was well below the level of the railway. The stone was lifted up to the railway by a hoist, the tower of which can clearly be seen. In 1944, to tap reserves of ironstone, an adit was driven into the quarry face and the hoist was used for this also. In May 1958 the nearby Thisleton Ironstone Mine opened, and extraction here ended.

Part of the Midland Railway, the railway line here closed completely on 28 February 1959, along with much of the Midland and Great Northern Railway, with which this line made an end on junction at Little Bytham.

Edenham

The Station, South Witham.

SOUTH LINCOLNSHIRE

One of the County's most unusual and short lived railway lines was that which served the Grimsthorpe Estate. It was built, owned and operated by one man, Baron Willoughby de Eresby, who lived at Grimsthorpe Castle. It ran from the nearest railway station, at Little Bytham, for four miles to Edenham. Opened for goods in 1855, it replaced a road between the two termini built in 1852. From 1857 to 1866 it carried passengers and it closed as long ago as 1873.

It was worked by three, by later standards, very primitive locomotives until 1872 from when it was horse worked. In addition to serving the needs of the Estate it also served Bourne, three miles to the east. In 1860, however, Bourne was reached by rail from Essendine and this reduced the traffic at Edenham.

This photograph (previous page), taken about 1970, shows the station at Edenham. The platform, which was covered by a canopy, was on the far side of the building. Small in scale, the building is typical of the line's buildings; built of limestone, with a clay pantiled roof along the ridge of which runs a row of decorated ridge tiles.

Rippingale Station is seen here in 1914. Authorised by an Act of 1865, the Great Northern Railway sought power to abandon the line in 1868. This was refused and the line, between Bourne and Sleaford, opened in 1872. The station lost its passenger service on 22 September 1930. A very early closure, quite an event at the time, as 99 stations nationwide, and 17 lines, were closed on that day. The line and the station remained open for goods and special passenger trains. The last of the latter was in 1951, when people were picked up here for a visit to the Festival of Britain. The line and the station closed completely on 15 June 1964, after having been busy, in its final years, with potatoes, grain and sugar beet.

Rippingale. Copyright O. King

Red Hall at Bourne is a fine early 17th Century house, restored as a museum in 1961-68, from its previous use as a Stationmaster's house and Booking Office. Surely, one of the stateliest railway stations in England. These two photographs show it in railway use and illustrate dramatic railway changes between the two dates.

The first railway to reach Bourne was the Bourn (sic) and Essendine Railway in 1860. Red Hall was purchased by them from the grandly named Sir Philip Duncombe - Pauncefort -

SOUTH LINCOLNSHIRE

Duncombe, Bart in that year and a small railway terminus was constructed alongside, with the building taken into its new use. In 1866 it became a through station with the opening of the line from Spalding. Passengers were catered for by a single platform alongside Red Hall and this can be seen in the first photograph, with carriages alongside.

The Red Hall, Bourne Station.

On the platform a fine early signal can be seen. Before the development of the Block System, which ensured that only one train could occupy a stretch of line at a time, trains were operated on a time interval system. In other words, signals were at danger for a few minutes after a train had passed before another train would be allowed to follow. Signals tended to be sited only at stations and junctions and were often bi-directional, as these are. That is, both directions were signalled from one post.

The Red Hall, Bourne Station.

In 1872 Bourne was linked to Sleaford by rail and a further platform had to be built. In 1893, with the construction of the line westwards to Saxby, there were major changes. The station was now to be on one of the country's main east - west routes, linking all of Norfolk with the Midlands, the Midland and Great Northern Joint Railway.

There was great concern in the town about the possible fate of Red Hall, and in 1893 a Memorial was drawn up. It was signed by 31 of the most influential residents of Bourne and the neighbourhood, seeking the preservation of the building. It was

SOUTH LINCOLNSHIRE

The Railway Station, Bourne.

retained and the station was rebuilt with the original platform removed, and a new island platform, reached by the new footbridge shown in the second photograph (overleaf). It was also at this time that the spelling of the station name was altered, with the final 'e' added to Bourne.

Passenger trains ceased running to Bourne from 28 February 1959, but goods trains ran between Spalding, Bourne and Billingborough for a further six years. The view above was taken shortly after the passenger trains stopped. Note that one of the line of rails leading to the west has been cut.

Certainly if regular trains were still running the boys could not sit here.

From left to right most of the railway infrastructure can be seen:- Bourne West signalbox, the engine shed, water tower, with Red Hall hidden behind, the platforms with the waiting rooms in front of the Church tower and, on the extreme right, the goods shed. On the platform is a bracket signal post, with the signals themselves having been removed.

Spalding Station opened in 1848. The first view shows it as it appeared at that time, from the south end. A

38

SOUTH LINCOLNSHIRE

Spalding, Station 1848, and later, pre 1900 photograph of almost the same view.

SOUTH LINCOLNSHIRE

double line of rails serves two platforms, the main one with the main buildings along its rear. Although Spalding is a town, the buildings are very similar to those provided for the country stations of the period. See the illustration of Bardney Station on page 15. The tall, square tower is a very distinctive feature of the Great Northern Railway of the period.

From these early beginnings Spalding grew in railway importance. From this station lines radiated like the spokes of a wheel. This line connected Boston to the north, with Peterborough to the south. In 1858 the line to Holbeach opened, in 1866 that to Bourne, followed in 1867 with the link to March and finally, that northwards to Sleaford in 1882.

All these extra trains, both passenger and goods, required a larger station at Spalding. The second view shows the station, again from the south. The two platforms have expanded to eight. The train is standing at Platform 2, used by trains heading to March. Platform 1 was the bay on the right, for trains for Holbeach and Sutton Bridge. Immediately to the left of the engine is Platform 3, for trains heading to Peterborough. The footbridge provides the link to Platforms 4,5,6, and 7. The original station buildings are hidden behind later extensions.

With the reduction in rail services things have come a full circle. Now a station on the Peterborough - Sleaford line, only the original platforms are in use today.

Railway Horse, Surfleet. Copyright A Turner

SOUTH LINCOLNSHIRE

Horses were always associated with railways. They were used for shunting sidings, hauling delivery drays and even, on some branch and mineral lines, as the prime motive power. At their peak in 1914, Britain's railways had almost 26000 horses in their service. On nationalisation in 1947, British Railways inherited 9000 of them. In 1967 the last was retired, having been working, appropriately, at Newmarket.

They were a common sight in Lincolnshire and this photograph shows one that was employed at Surfleet station, just north of Spalding, around the turn of the century.

When the railways first came to Lincolnshire there were no photographers around to record the events. We rely, therefore, on paintings and drawings. To mark the coming of the railway to Boston this lithograph was published in 1848. It shows a Great Northern Railway train approaching the bridge over the Witham, heading north.

This early bridge was built of timber and approached over a low viaduct. In 1850 the viaduct was replaced by an embankment, the bridge itself being replaced by the present Grand Sluice railway bridge in 1885. This later embankment and bridge were on a slightly different line, built to ease the

Boston, 1848.

sharp curve seen in the illustration and to provide a double line of rails.

Despite the detail of the locomotive it has not been possible to identify it exactly. It is a 2-2-2, a number of which the Great Northern Railway employed in its early days and which were later rebuilt. It is, however, typical of the engines of the period, with the crew occupying a very exposed position on the footplate. No provision was made for their shelter and they would have been expected to work a shift of twelve hours or more.

Boston Dock. Copyright Museum of English Rural Life

SOUTH LINCOLNSHIRE

Holbeach.

Boston Dock was opened in December 1884 and at the same time the River Witham between it and the sea was improved. From the first it was rail connected, as it still is today. This view is believed to have been taken during the Second World War and appears to show the transhipment of potatoes between ship and railway wagons.

Potatoes have been a major industry in South East Lincolnshire for many years. In the 1920s two to four hundred wagon loads were despatched a day. Farmers delivered their produce, in sacks, to the wayside stations, from where they were taken to Boston and Spalding. From here, trains were despatched all over the country and to the docks for export.

In 1916 the principal destinations were London, Newcastle, Leeds, Sheffield and Manchester, and to the docks at London, Hull, Southampton and Liverpool for export. Seed potatoes were brought from Scotland, both by sea and rail. This photograph most probably shows seed potatoes being unloaded, to be delivered to the farmers for an early spring sowing.

SOUTH LINCOLNSHIRE

The local railway station was a popular subject for Victorian and Edwardian picture postcards. In this one of Holbeach (previous page) in 1911, the town's railway station takes centre stage. The existence of a railway station was very important. It was the link to everywhere else, literally a global public transport network.

The Norwich and Spalding Railway opened the first section of their line, from Spalding to Holbeach on 3 May 1858. It took another four years before the line was extended to Sutton Bridge, a long time considering that there were no engineering problems on that nine mile single track line.

Probably the most important traffic at Holbeach was the produce of its farms. In common with other nearby stations, soon after Christmas flowers were despatched. In the spring cabbages, broccoli and salad crops were followed by soft fruits, gooseberries, red and black currants, raspberries and strawberries from June to August. As the year moved on peas, plums and apples were sent away, and potatoes and sugar beet followed in winter. Many of these crops were perishable and were sent by trains with express speeds to London and other markets.

The second railway in Lincolnshire, but only by two months, was the Midland Railway branch from Peterborough to Stamford, opened in October 1848. It was extended onwards to Melton Mowbray fifteen months later. The town was given a station befitting the town's glorious architecture, seen here in this double view. The two views are taken from a slightly differing point. The reason for this is that this was produced, in the earlier part of this century, for 3D viewing.

The building is in a Tudor style, built in 1848 and designed by an architect named Sancton Wood. On the left, below the octagonal turret, is the Waiting Room; in the centre the

Stamford Station.

SOUTH LINCOLNSHIRE

Stamford East. Copyright Author

Booking Office and, to the right, the two storey Stationmaster's house. On top of the turret is a weathervane, comprising the letters SPR, the initials of the promoting company, the Stamford and Peterborough Railway.

Happily, the station is still used by trains and the former house is a bookshop, selling one of the finest selection of railway books in the country. The railway line itself has little influence on the appearance of the town, to the left of this view it enters a tunnel to take it underneath the old Great North Road.

The town's second station has been long converted into flats and is shown in the second photograph. The area's greatest landowner and a member of one of the greatest families in the land was the Marquess of Exeter. He did not want railways near to his home, Burghley House, and its park. There was also great concern about the railways taking away one of the town's greatest industries, the coaching trade.

As a result, the main line to the north and to London, was built four miles to the east and Tallington Station was linked to the town with a horse bus service.

The Marquess, and the townspeople soon realised their mistake and a line was promoted to link Stamford with Essendine. It opened in November 1856, and was joined with a second line, south to Wansford, in 1867. Together known as the Marquess of Exeters Railway, they had their own terminus in Stamford, on Water Street, known in later years as Stamford East.

Inspired by Burghley House and designed by William Hurst, in a Tudor style, with a square tower at the rear, the building displays a Coat of Arms on each front wing, those of the Marquess and of the Town. The station offices were on the ground floor and on the first floor were the Stationmaster's accommodation, together with, in the left hand wing, a Boardroom and Secretary's Office.

The line to Wansford closed as long ago as 1929, and that to Essendine in 1959. East Station had closed prior to this, on 4 March 1957, from which time trains were transferred to the town's other station. It was converted to two houses. The platforms and lines at the rear were demolished and in 1987 new houses were put up in their place.